THE QUEEN

365 POSITIVE AFFIRMATIONS
FOR BLACK WOMEN

INSPIRE
TODAY
PRESS

you are a queen

YOU ARE BEAUTIFUL, LOVED AND CONFIDENT. YOU HAVE THE POWER TO OVERCOME YOUR PAST AND FACE YOUR FUTURE WITHOUT FEAR. YOU ARE A QUEEN.

THIS BOOK IS A GUIDE FOR YOUR NEXT 365 DAYS. THERE IS A CHAPTER FOR EVERY CHALLENGE AND SEASON OF LIFE.

THESE DAILY AFFIRMATIONS WILL ASSIST YOU ON YOUR JOURNEY TO UNLEASH THE QUEEN WITHIN. DON'T LET ANYONE OR ANYTHING STOP YOU BUT BE RELENTLESS DAILY IN SPEAKING THESE AFFIRMATIONS OVER YOUR LIFE AND BE AMAZED HOW YOUR LIFE CHANGES.

contents page

WEALTH 1-4
ABUNDANCE 5-8
BUSINESS 9-12
LEGACY 13-16
TRAVEL 17-20
LEARNING 21-24
RELATIONSHIPS 25-28
MARRIAGE 29-32
FAMILY 33-36
LOVE 37-40
SELF CARE 41-44
HEALTH & FITNESS 45-48
CAREER 49-52
TIME 53-56
PASSION 57-60
WORRY/ANXIETY 61-64
FEAR 65-68
MY PAST 69-72
MY PRESENT 73-76
MY FUTURE 77-80
MINDFULNESS 81-84
PRODUCTIVITY 85-88
FOOD/COOKING 89-96

wealth

1. I AM THANKFUL FOR
ALL OF THE BLESSINGS
IN MY LIFE.

2. MY THOUGHTS ARE ON
ENDLESS AFFLUENCE
AND ABUNDANCE.

3. I RECEIVE NEW
BLESSINGS ON A
REGULAR BASIS.

4. MY ABILITIES AND
GIFTS ARE HIGHLY
RESPECTED, AND THEY
HELP ME MAKE A LOT OF
MONEY.

5. POSITIVE ENERGY
FLOWS FREELY AND
CONTINUALLY THROUGH
ME.

6. I HAVE THE FORESIGHT TO MANAGE VAST SUMS OF MONEY PROPERLY.

7. ON A REGULAR BASIS, I RECEIVE BOTH EXPECTED AND UNEXPECTED BLESSINGS.

8. IN MY LIFE, I AM MANIFESTING MIRACLES.

9. PROSPERITY, RICHNESS, AND JOY ABOUND IN MY LIFE.

10. I HAVE LIMITLESS MONEY-MAKING POTENTIAL.

11. I HAVE AN ABUNDANCE OF OPPORTUNITIES THAT HAVE ENRICHED MY LIFE.

12. I AM FORTUNATE TO BE ABLE TO BLESS OTHERS.

13. EVERY DAY, I IMPROVE MY FINANCIAL SITUATION.

14. MY FORTUNE CONTINUES TO RISE BECAUSE I INVEST INTELLIGENTLY.

15. I'VE LET GO OF ALL FINANCIAL ANXIETIES AND DOUBTS.

abundance

16. I AM THE OWNER OF ALL WEALTH.

17. I AM DESERVING OF EVERYTHING THAT LIFE HAS TO GIVE.

18. IN EVERY ASPECT OF MY LIFE, I ANTICIPATE AN IMPROVEMENT.

19. PROSPERITY, WEALTH, AND INCREDIBLE HEALTH ARE ALL COMING INTO MY LIFE.

20. MY DESTINY IS TO BE PROSPEROUS.

21. I AM A PRICELESS GEM WHO IS DESERVING OF ALL THAT THIS PLANET HAS TO GIVE.

22. I MANIFEST LUXURY IN ALL OF ITS FORMS, AS WELL AS CALM AND HAPPINESS.

23. I AM DESERVING OF THIS LIFE OF LUXURY AND PLENTY.

24. I MAKE ENOUGH MONEY TO LIVE THE LIFESTYLE I WANT AND THEN SOME.

25. BY DECLARING PROSPERITY OVER MY LIFE, I AM PROSPERING.

26. IN MY LIFE, I ANNOUNCE PROSPERITY AND ABUNDANCE.

27. I'M ATTRACTING GOOD FORTUNE TO MYSELF.

28. MY THOUGHTS AND NEW VISION ARE FUELED BY MY CREATIVE ENERGY.

29. I ALREADY HAVE EVERYTHING I NEED TO LIVE THE LIFE I WANT.

30. I HAVE BOUNDLESS WEALTH-CREATION POTENTIAL.

business

31. I AM DESERVING OF SUCCESS, AND I AM EAGER TO PURSUE MY GOALS!

32. I'M REALLY LOOKING FORWARD TO SEEING WHERE THIS ADVENTURE TAKES ME AND MEETING ALL OF THE LOVELY LIKE-MINDED FOLKS I'LL ENCOUNTER ALONG THE WAY!

33. I PUT A LOT OF GOOD ENERGY INTO MY BUSINESS, AND I'M DESERVING OF HAVING IT RETURNED TO ME MULTIPLIED.

34. I POSSESS THE ABILITIES REQUIRED TO BUILD A PROFITABLE COMPANY.

35. I BEAR THE NECESSARY SKILLS FOR SUCCESS.

36. I'M DEDICATED TO MY OBJECTIVES, PERSONAL DEVELOPMENT, AND MISSION!

37. I BELIEVE I AM DESERVING OF SUCCESS, AND I AM PREPARED TO PURSUE MY AMBITIONS!

38. WHEN I BRING MY TRUE SELF TO WORK, I GET REWARDED FINANCIALLY.

39. I CAN ACCOMPLISH EVERYTHING I SET MY MIND TO FOR MY COMPANY.

40. IN THE YEAR 2022, I WILL EXPERIENCE MY MOST PROFITABLE MONTHS.

41. I CARRY OUT MY BUSINESS STRATEGIES WITH CLARITY AND VISION.

42. MY RESPONSIBILITIES ARE PRIORITIZED, AND I STICK TO MY BUSINESS PLAN.

43. I'M TAKING DAILY STEPS TO MAKE MY BUSINESS A REALITY.

44. MY COMPANY IS SET UP TO WORK WITH THE IDEAL CLIENTS FOR OUR VIBE.

45. I PROVIDE EXCEPTIONAL VALUE THROUGH MY BUSINESS.

legacy

46. I AM COGNIZANT OF MY LIFE'S IMPORTANCE.

47. FULFILLING MY LIFE'S PATH BRINGS ME JOY.

48. I DEVOTE MY TIME TO MY LIFE'S LEGACY.

49. I ELIMINATE ALL DUTIES UNRELATED TO MY LEGACY.

50. I AM DETERMINED TO CONTINUE ON MY LIFE'S PATH.

51. I FOCUS MY TIME AND ATTENTION ON REALIZING MY LIFE'S LEGACY.

52. MY LEGACY IS IMPACTFUL AND IMPORTANT.

53. I LIVE IN THE MOMENT WHILE SIMULTANEOUSLY MOVING TOWARDS THE FUTURE.

54. I AM PROUD OF THE LEGACY THAT I AM BUILDING.

55. I AM CHOSEN TO CREATE A LEGACY WORTH LEAVING.

56. I AM DELIBERATELY PRIORITIZING MY ACTIONS TO REACH MY FUTURE GOALS.

57. I WORK DILIGENTLY EACH DAY WITH PRIDE TO ACHIEVE MY DREAMS.

58. THE FOUNDATION I AM LAYING TODAY IMPACTS THE PEOPLE OF TOMORROW.

59. I MAKE RESPONSIBLE DECISIONS ABOUT THE USE OF MY TIME.

60. I ENJOY THE LIFE THAT I AM LIVING AND THE FUTURE I AM CREATING.

travel

61. MY CONCEPT OF SELF-CARE AND RELAXATION IS TO TRAVEL.

62. I AM READY TO TRAVEL AND SEE THE WORLD.

63. I AM OPEN TO NEW EXPERIENCES.

64. I HAVE THE FREEDOM TO GO WHEREVER I WANT WHENEVER I WANT.

65. TRAVEL IS A LUXURY THAT I CONSIDER ESSENTIAL IN LIVING MY BEST LIFE.

66. I LET GO OF WHATEVER FEARS, WORRIES, OR CONCERNS I HAVE ABOUT MY SAFETY ALONG THE JOURNEY.

67. AT HOME AND ABROAD, I AM SAFE.

68. REGARDLESS OF WHAT IS GOING ON IN THE WORLD, I AM PREDESTINED FOR PURPOSE AND ACHIEVEMENT.

69. I AM LOOKING FORWARD TO MY NEXT TRIP.

70. TRAVELING BRINGS ME JOY AND PEACE.

71. EVERY OPPORTUNITY TO TRAVEL WILL BE TAKEN ADVANTAGE OF.

72. ONLY THE MOST FAVORABLE TRAVEL OPTIONS ARE OFFERED TO ME.

73. I AM MORE GRATEFUL THAN EVER TO BE ABLE TO TRAVEL.

74. I'VE CHOSEN TO BE AT EASE AND ENJOY THE RIDE.

75. I AM ONLY DIRECTED TO THE APPROPRIATE LOCATIONS FOR ME.

Learning

76. MY MIND IS RECEPTIVE TO NEW CONCEPTS.

77. I'M MORE FOCUSED AND CLEAR THAN I'VE EVER BEEN.

78. I HAVE A THOROUGH COMPREHENSION OF DIFFICULT IDEAS.

79. I AM A MASTER OF CONCENTRATION.

80. I EMBRACE THE RICHNESS OF KNOWLEDGE BEING IMPARTED TO ME.

81. I ATTRACT NEW INFORMATION LIKE A MAGNET.

82. I AM ABLE TO RETAIN INFORMATION QUICKLY AND READILY.

83. I AM A DEDICATED AND STUDIOUS INDIVIDUAL.

84. I PLACE A HIGH PRIORITY ON EDUCATION AND COMPREHENSION.

85. EVERY DAY, I DEVOTE TIME TO STUDYING.

86. MY MIND IS A MARVEL.

87. I'M WELL-VERSED AND WELL-EQUIPPED.

88. EVERYTHING I LEARN IS PROCESSED QUICKLY IN MY HEAD.

89. I AM A FANTASTIC STUDENT.

90. I ADORE LEARNING NEW THINGS!

relationships

91. I VALUE POSITIVE, INTIMATE RELATIONSHIPS.

92. I MAINTAIN STRONG, CLOSE BONDS WITH OTHERS.

93. I CHERISH GENUINE, HONEST RELATIONSHIPS WITH FRIENDS AND FAMILY.

94. I ATTRACT LOVING, NONTOXIC RELATIONSHIPS.

95. IN MY RELATIONSHIPS, I GIVE AND RECEIVE LOVE AS WELL AS RESPECT.

96. I ADORE AND ACCEPT
MY MATE, FLAWS AND ALL.

97. I AM DETERMINED TO
IMPROVE MY CONNECTIONS.

98. I AM THE MASTER OF
MY OWN HAPPINESS.

99. I AM DESERVING OF
LOVE.

100. I ATTRACT THE TYPE
OF RELATIONSHIPS I
DESIRE.

101. I HAVE EARNED THE
RIGHT TO LOVE AND BE
LOVED.

102. I DESERVE A LONG-
TERM, HAPPY, AND
FULFILLING RELATIONSHIP.

103. I HAVE SOLID, LOVING,
AND COMMITTED
RELATIONSHIPS.

104. EVERY DAY, MY
FEELINGS AND
CONNECTIONS ARE
GROWING STRONGER.

105. I AM A GREAT
LISTENER AND
COMMUNICATOR.

marriage

106. I'M THANKFUL THAT MY HUSBAND AND I AGREE ON OUR PLANS FOR THE FUTURE.

107. MY HUSBAND AND I COLLABORATE TO ATTAIN OUR OBJECTIVES.

108. I AM GRATEFUL FOR MY HUSBAND, AND MARRYING HIM REMAINS THE BEST DECISION I HAVE EVER MADE.

109. MY SPOUSE AND I ARE AN IRRESISTIBLE FORCE TO BE RECKONED WITH IN EVERY MANNER.

110. MY HUBBY IS SOMEONE I ADORE AND ADMIRE. HE IS A WONDERFUL MAN WHO ADORES OUR FAMILY AND OFFERS EVERYTHING WE REQUIRE.

111. MY HUSBAND AND I MAKE A CONSCIOUS EFFORT TO LOVE EACH OTHER ON A DAILY BASIS.

112. I ADMIRE AND RESPECT MY PARTNER FOR WHAT THEY CONTRIBUTE TO OUR MARRIAGE.

113. MY PARTNER AND I ARE VERY MUCH IN LOVE.

114. I AM COMPLETELY DEVOTED TO MY PARTNER.

115. I BELIEVE IN OUR RELATIONSHIP.

116. OUR UNION IS NOTHING SHORT OF A MIRACLE.

117. LOVE, TRUST, AND SUPPORT ARE THE FOUNDATIONS OF MY MARRIAGE.

118. I LOVE AND RESPECT MY SPOUSE UNCONDITIONALLY.

119. EVERY SINGLE DAY, WE SHOW UP IN OUR MARRIAGE.

120. I GENUINELY RESPECT AND TRUST MY LIFE PARTNER.

family

121. MY FAMILY AND I MUTUALLY ADORE ONE ANOTHER.

122. I AM FORTUNATE TO HAVE A LOVING AND SUPPORTIVE FAMILY.

123. MY ENTIRE FAMILY IS CONTENT AND HEALTHY.

124. EVERYONE IN MY LIFE COMMUNICATES WITH EACH OTHER IN AN OPEN AND HONEST MANNER.

125. MY FAMILY MEMBERS ARE TRUSTWORTHY AND CARING.

126. I AM DEDICATED TO MY FAMILY.

127. MY FAMILY AND I UNDERSTAND ONE ANOTHER WELL.

128. WE SHARE UNBREAKABLE BONDS THAT ENHANCE OUR LIVES IN THE OUTSIDE WORLD.

129. MY FAMILY IS PROSPERING.

130. I AM PROUD TO BE A PART OF MY FAMILY.

131. I AM BLESSED TO HAVE A FAMILY WHO IS SUCCEEDING IN LIFE.

132. MY FAMILY IS PROSPEROUS.

133. MY FAMILY IS OVERFLOWING IN LOVE AND RESPECT.

134. MY FAMILY ACCEPTS ME FOR WHO I AM.

135. I ENJOY SPENDING TIME WITH MY FAMILY.

love

136. I ENJOY GETTING TO KNOW AND LOVE MYSELF ENTIRELY.

137. I ADORE BEING A STUNNING, INTELLIGENT BLACK WOMAN.

138. KINDNESS, RESPECT, AND PROTECTION ARE ALL THINGS I DESERVE.

139. I PLACE A HIGH VALUE ON MY FULL EXISTENCE AND REFUSE TO ACCEPT ANYTHING LESS.

140. I AM A BRONZE GODDESS WHO IS LOVELY AND CARING.

141. I AM PROUD OF MY BRAVERY AND STRENGTH.

142. LOVING MYSELF IS A NEED IN MY LIFE.

143. I WALK IN MY OWN TRUTH AND LET GO OF OTHER PEOPLE'S IDEAS.

144. I AM COMPLETELY ENAMORED WITH MYSELF.

145. I'M EVEN MORE IN LOVE WITH WHO I'M BECOMING.

146. I CONSCIOUSLY AND COMPLETELY LOVE MYSELF.

147. I PLACE A HIGH VALUE ON MYSELF.

148. EVERY DAY, I MAKE THE DECISION TO HONOR MYSELF.

149. RECEIVING AFFECTION AND RESPECT IS SOMETHING I'M VERY ENTHUSIASTIC ABOUT.

150. LOVE EXISTS IN ME AND IS A PART OF WHO I AM.

self-care

151. I AM SUCCESSFUL, POWERFUL, AND TENACIOUS.

152. I AM THE BEST INVESTMENT I CAN MAKE IN MYSELF.

153. I FOCUS ON MY PERSONAL OBJECTIVES AND ALLOW MYSELF TO DREAM.

154. ONE OF THE WAYS I SHOW MYSELF LOVE IS BY TAKING CARE OF MYSELF.

155. I SET ASIDE TIME TO ATTEND TO MY PERSONAL REQUIREMENTS.

156. I DEVOTE TIME AND EFFORT TO CULTIVATING LOVING RELATIONSHIPS WITH MYSELF AND OTHERS.

157. I PLACE A HIGH SIGNIFICANCE ON MY OWN DISTINCT VIEWPOINTS AND INSIGHTS.

158. AS PART OF MY SELF-CARE PRACTICE, I ESTABLISH APPROPRIATE LIMITS.

159. I REFUSE TO GIVE UP ON MYSELF WHEN THINGS GET TOUGH.

160. I REFUSE TO CONFORM TO OTHERS' EXPECTATIONS.

161. I RESPECT MY TIME TO REST AND ENSURE THAT I HAVE ENOUGH TIME TO REJUVENATE.

162. MY AUTHENTIC SELF IS SOMETHING I VALUE AND RESPECT.

163. I CHERISH EVERY ASPECT OF MY BEING AND RECOGNIZE MY WORTH.

164. I REFUSE TO LET THE OPINIONS OF OTHERS DICTATE MY SELF WORTH.

165. I EMBRACE MY AUTHENTIC SELF, WHICH PRODUCES A NATURAL BEAUTY THAT CANNOT BE DILUTED BY THE WORLD.

health & fitness

166. I AM IN GOOD HEALTH, AM CONTENT, AND AM PROSPEROUS.

167. I AM FEARLESS, POWERFUL, AND SUCCESSFUL.

168. EVERY DAY, I MAKE EXCELLENT DIETARY AND EXERCISE CHOICES.

169. I AM THANKFUL FOR MY GOOD HEALTH, PEACE, AND HAPPINESS.

170. TODAY'S DECISIONS ARE BOLSTERING MY CHANCES FOR TOMORROW'S SUCCESS.

171. TO FEED MY BODY, I EAT THE CORRECT FOODS.

172. MY MIND AND BODY ARE BOTH HEALING AT THE MOMENT.

173. I RECOGNIZE THE PROPER NUTRITION AND ACTIVITIES THAT BRING LIFE TO MY BODY.

174. I AM IN TUNE WITH WHAT SPECIFICALLY WORKS FOR ME.

175. I ONLY CONSUME THE BEST, MOST NUTRITIOUS FOODS.

176. I CHOOSE THE PROPER FOODS TO PROMOTE HEALTH AND STRENGTH.

177. I TREAT MY BODY WELL BECAUSE IT IS MY TEMPLE.

178. I HONOR MY BODY WITH MOVEMENT.

179. I AM FLEXIBLE, AGILE, AND ENJOY A FULL RANGE OF MOTION.

180. I AM BLESSED, WHOLE, AND CONSISTENT.

career

181. MY PROFESSIONAL LIFE IS A JOURNEY THAT I AM ENJOYING.

182. I TRUST MY PROFESSIONAL PATH.

183. I AM IN CHARGE OF MY CAREER'S DESTINATION.

184. I AM CONFIDENT IN MY CAREER OBJECTIVES AND KNOW WHAT I AM STRIVING FOR.

185. I AM FULLY CAPABLE OF ACCOMPLISHING MY CAREER GOALS.

186. I AM CLEAR ON MY VISION FOR MY CAREER.

187. MY CAREER SUITS ME WELL.

188. I AM EXCITED ABOUT MY PROFESSIONAL LIFE.

189. I HAVE A FULFILLING LIFE OVERALL AND MY CAREER IS EXCEPTIONAL.

190. I AM DETERMINED TO PURSUE MY PROFESSIONAL PASSIONS UNAPOLOGETICALLY.

191. I AM DESERVING OF SUCCESS.

192. I AM GETTING CLOSER TO MY OBJECTIVES WITH EACH STEP I TAKE.

193. MY ABILITY TO SUCCEED IS INFINITE.

194. I KNOW EXACTLY WHAT I NEED TO DO TO BE SUCCESSFUL.

195. MY CONTRIBUTION TO THE WORLD IS SIGNIFICANT.

time

196. TIME IS WORKING ON MY BEHALF.

197. I HAVE IMPECCABLE TIMING.

198. I HAVE A GIFT FOR RECOGNIZING THE BEST TIMING FOR ME.

199. I AM ALWAYS IN ALIGNMENT WITH OPPORTUNITIES.

200. TIME HAS THE TENDENCY TO BE ON MY SIDE.

201. I AM EXCELLENT AT MANAGING MY TIME.

202. I AM MORE EFFICIENT WITH MY TIME THAN EVER BEFORE.

203. TIME IS BECOMING ONE OF MY ALLIES.

204. I HAVE A REPUTATION FOR COMPLETING MY ASSIGNMENTS ON TIME.

205. ALL OF THE IDEAS I REQUIRE ARRIVE AT PRECISELY THE CORRECT TIME.

206. MY TIME IS NOW!

207. I TEND TO MEET THE CORRECT INDIVIDUALS AT THE RIGHT TIME.

208. I HAVE ALL THE TIME THAT I NEED.

209. I AM RELAXED AND FREE TO USE MY TIME WISELY.

210. I HAVE ENOUGH TIME TO WORK EFFECTIVELY WHILE ENJOYING MY LIFE.

passion

211. WITH MY PASSION, THE IMPOSSIBLE IS POSSIBLE.

212. I POSSESS THE PASSION TO ACCOMPLISH GREAT THINGS.

213. I AM DRIVEN TO MOVE OUTSIDE OF MY COMFORT ZONE THIS YEAR.

214. MY DREAMS ARE ENORMOUS!

215. I AM A VISIONARY FULL OF PASSION.

216. MY ZEAL FOR LIFE IS UNMATCHED.

217. I AM PASSIONATE ABOUT MY LIFE'S MISSION.

218. I AM CAPABLE OF LIVING A LARGE, MAGNANIMOUS LIFE.

219. I REFUSE TO SHRINK BACK AND PLAY SMALL.

220. I PLAN TO FULFILL EVERY GOAL I SET FORTH.

221. I REFUSE TO HOLD BACK ON MY DREAMS.

222. I BELIEVE IN MY VISION SO MUCH THAT IT IS BECOMING MY REALITY.

223. THE ESSENCE OF MY BEING IS EXUDING PASSION.

224. I AM COURAGEOUS AND READY TO PURSUE MY DESTINY.

225. I BEHOLD AN ENDURING WISDOM AND PASSION THAT COMES FROM THE ROYAL LINEAGE OF QUEENS BEFORE ME.

worry/
anxiety

226. EVERY DAY, I KEEP MY MIND ENGAGED WITH APPRECIATION.

227. I AM DESERVING OF AN EXTRAORDINARY LIFE.

228. I SPEAK HIGHLY OF MYSELF AND MY AMBITIONS TO LIVE THE LIFE I DESERVE.

229. I TAKE A DEEP BREATH OF TRANQUILITY AND LET GO OF MY WORRIES.

230. I EXORCISE FEAR AND SKEPTICISM REGULARLY.

231. I LIVE A LIFE THAT IS MEANINGFUL TO ME!

232. IN BOTH MY PERSONAL AND PROFESSIONAL ENDEAVORS, I AM CALM.

233. I'M HAPPY TO SAY THAT I'VE MADE PEACE WITH MY PAST.

234. I TRUST THAT PEACE WILL GUIDE ME IN THE RIGHT DIRECTION.

235. I ALLOW MYSELF TO BE FREE AND AT EASE.

236. I EXUDE CALM AND
OPENNESS TO NEW
OPPORTUNITIES.

237. I ALLOW TRANQUILITY
TO PERVADE ALL ASPECTS
OF MY BEING.

238. MY BODY IS RELAXED
AND ECSTATICALLY
OPTIMISTIC.

239. I DRAW LOVING, CALM
ENERGY TO MYSELF.

240. I WALK IN
CONFIDENCE AND POWER.

fear

241. MY BRAVERY IS BIGGER THAN ANY FEAR I MAY HAVE.

242. I AM CONFIDENT IN MY SAFETY.

243. I BELIEVE EVERYTHING WILL ALWAYS WORK OUT FOR ME.

244. I AM APPRECIATIVE, SO MY MIND IS CLEAR.

245. I HAVE CONTROL OVER MY EMOTIONS.

246. I'M GOING TO PUSH
BEYOND MY FEAR AND
MOVE FORWARD.

247. I'M GOING TO
SURROUND MYSELF WITH
POSITIVITY AND LOVE.

248. I CAN FIND JOY IN
THE SMALLEST OF THINGS.

249. I AM FREE TO CREATE
THE LIFE I DESIRE TO LIVE.

250. I REFUSE TO BE HELD
CAPTIVE BY FEAR.

251. THIS FEAR AND ANXIETY IS UNFOUNDED.

252. I AM FREE TO FOCUS ON MY OWN UNIQUE DESTINY.

253. I HAVE THE COURAGE TO TAKE MY OWN UNIQUE PATH. I RELEASE ALL FEARS AND DOUBTS.

254. I AM FULL OF PURPOSE, VISION, AND ABILITY.

255. I STAND FIRMLY IN MY TRUTH AND HOLD MY HEAD HIGH AS I BOLDLY MAKE MY DREAMS MY REALITY.

my past

256. MY PAST IS BEHIND ME AND I AM VICTORIOUS.

257. I FORGIVE MYSELF AND EVICT ALL PAST HURTS AND SHAME THAT HAVE ATTACHED TO MY LIFE.

258. I VALUE MY PRIOR SUCCESSES AND USE THEM AS BUILDING STONES FOR FUTURE SUCCESSES!

259. IN MY MIND, BODY, AND SPIRIT, I AM ENTIRELY HEALED FROM THE PAST.

260. I HAVE FORGIVEN MYSELF AS WELL AS OTHERS.

261. ALL OF MY PREVIOUS TOXIC RELATIONSHIPS HAVE COME TO AN END.

262. I AM FREE OF SADNESS, HURT, PAIN, OR DEFEAT.

263. I AM ACCEPTED.

264. I POSSESS A NEW ENTHUSIASM ABOUT LIFE.

265. I CHOOSE TO BE TRUE TO MYSELF.

266. MY HISTORY DOES NOT DICTATE MY PRESENT NOR FUTURE OUTCOMES.

267. I AM FREE OF THE OPINIONS OF OTHERS. THE MOST IMPORTANT THING IS MY IMPRESSION OF MYSELF.

268. I AM AT EASE AND CONFIDENT IN MY OWN SKIN.

269. EVERY TERRIBLE EVENT I'VE HAD IN THE PAST HAS BEEN TURNED INTO AN ADVANTAGE FOR MY FUTURE.

270. I AM RESOLVED TO RECLAIM MY PEACE OF MIND, LOVE, AND HAPPINESS.

my present

271. I AM FULLY PRESENT
IN MY LIFE.

272. I SHOW UP EACH AND
EVERY DAY TO LIVE LIFE TO
THE FULLEST.

273. I AM THE PINNACLE OF
BLACK ACHIEVEMENT.

274. WITH BRAVERY,
ELEGANCE, AND GRACE, I
WEAR MY CROWN PROUDLY.

275. I BRING GIFTS AND
BRILLIANCE THAT CHANGE
THE ENVIRONMENT.

276. I AM GENEROUS AT EVERY OPPORTUNITY.

277. I AM GRATEFUL FOR MY FULL, RICH, AND PROSPEROUS LIFE.

278. MY INTELLECTUAL PROPERTY IS MORE VALUABLE THAN ALL THE WORLD'S WEALTH COMBINED.

279. EVERY DAY, I CELEBRATE MY BLACKNESS.

280. REGARDLESS OF THE WORLD'S INEQUITY, I AM DESERVING OF RESPECT AND AFFECTION.

281. RATHER THAN MISGIVINGS, I AM GUIDED BY MY DREAMS.

282. I'M MORE THAN A VICTOR!

283. I AM EXCITED AND PROUD TO EMBARK ON THIS PATH KNOWN AS "LIFE."

284. EVERY CHANCE I GET TO WALK IN MY PURPOSE IS ONE I TREASURE.

285. I'M DEDICATED TO ACHIEVING MY OWN GOALS.

my future

286. MY BLACKNESS SHOULD BE RECOGNIZED AND CELEBRATED.

287. I AM ADAMANT ABOUT OCCUPYING MY SEAT AT THE TABLE.

288. WINNING IS IN MY BLOOD.

289. MY PROFESSION IS A FANTASTIC MATCH FOR ME. I'M PROUD OF WHAT I'VE ACHIEVED!

290. MONEY COMES TO ME WITH EASE.

291. I MAKE RISKY FINANCIAL DECISIONS THAT BENEFIT ME.

292. I'M RESOURCEFUL WHEN IT COMES TO GENERATING MULTIPLE STREAMS OF MONEY.

293. I HAVE AN ABUNDANCE OF RESOURCES AT MY DISPOSAL TO HELP ME ACHIEVE MY GOALS.

294. MY SUPPORT SYSTEM IS LARGE AND STRONG.

295. MY WEALTH IS INCREASING ON A DAILY BASIS.

296. I AM A NECESSARY
PART OF THIS WORLD.

297. MY WEALTH EXPANDS
AS I CONTRIBUTE.

298. I'M IN GOOD HEALTH
AND HAVE A LOT OF MONEY.

299. I AM GLAD FOR A LIFE
THAT IS FULL, WEALTHY,
AND SUCCESSFUL.

300. MY CONTRIBUTIONS
ARE IMPACTFUL.

mindfulness

301. I HAVE ARRIVED.

302. I AM FIRMLY PLANTED
IN THE PRESENT.

303. I AM IN THE ROOM.

304. I AM FIRMLY PLANTED.

305. RIGHT NOW, I HAVE
ALL I REQUIRE.

306. I AM EXACTLY WHERE I'M SUPPOSED TO BE.

307. I AM VERY SAFE AND SECURE.

308. I AM A STRONG, STABLE, AND GROUNDED INDIVIDUAL.

309. I AM MEANT FOR THIS EXACT MOMENT.

310. I AM THANKFUL FOR THE BREATH THAT ENTERS MY LUNGS.

311. I AM AT PEACE,
GROUNDED, AND
CONFIDENT.

312. I FEEL THAT THIS IS
EXACTLY HOW IT'S
SUPPOSED TO BE.

313. I HAVE EVERYTHING
THAT I EXPECTED.

314. I AM LOOKING AT THE
WORLD WITH NEW EYES.

315. I AM FULLY ALIGNED.

productivity

316. I AM CONFIDENT IN MY ABILITIES AND IN MY ABILITY TO SUCCEED.

317. I AM CREATIVE IN ALL THAT I DO.

318. IDEAS AND NEW CONCEPTS FLOW TO ME EASILY.

319. I AM EFFICIENT AT MY WORK.

320. I AM ALWAYS PONDERING NEW SYSTEMS TO IMPROVE MY PRODUCTIVITY.

321. I ENJOY MY WORK SO IT COMES NATURALLY TO ME.

322. I AM IN A HARMONIOUS FLOW OF PRODUCTIVITY.

323. I AM A UNIQUE CREATOR.

324. I DEVOTE TIME AND ENERGY TO MY PRIORITIES.

325. MY WORK IS IMPACTFUL.

326. I AM IN COMMAND.

327. I AM CONFIDENT IN MYSELF AND MY ABILITIES.

328. MY PAST WINS PROVIDE THE MOTIVATION NEEDED TO SURPASS MY OWN EXPECTATIONS.

329. I REFUSE TO MAKE EXCUSES.

330. I FIGURE OUT WAYS TO OVERCOME ALL OBSTACLES.

food/ cooking

331. I AM THANKFUL FOR A HEALTHY RELATIONSHIP WITH FOOD.

332. FOOD IS NECESSARY TO FUEL MY BODY.

333. I MAKE EXCELLENT LIFESTYLE CHOICES.

334. I CONSCIOUSLY EAT TO STAY ALIVE AND HEALTHY.

335. I HAVE A LOVING RELATIONSHIP WITH FOOD AND ENJOY EVERY BITE.

336. MY FOOD AWARENESS IS GUIDED BY MY BODY.

337. I AM LISTENING TO MY BODY.

338. I AM ENTHRALLED BY THE FLAVORS AND TEXTURES OF THIS MEAL.

339. I AM CHOOSING TO BE GENTLE TO MYSELF.

340. WHEN I AM JUST SATISFIED, I QUIT EATING.

341. I EAT HEALTHILY IN ORDER TO LIVE WELL.

342. I AM GRATEFUL FOR THE PROVISION OF FOOD.

343. I AM FREE FROM NEGATIVE FOOD-RELATED BEHAVIORS AND HABITS.

344. I AM THANKFUL TO HAVE ACCESS TO HEALTHY FOODS.

345. I CHOOSE THE RIGHT FOODS TO KEEP ME ENERGIZED.

346. COOKING BRINGS ME
JOY.

347. ONE OF THE MAIN
INGREDIENTS IN MY DISHES
IS LOVE.

348. I CREATE UNIQUE,
APPETIZING MEALS.

349. MY MEALS ARE
BALANCED AND
NOURISHING.

350. MY KITCHEN IS MY
SANCTUARY.

351. RELATIONSHIPS ARE BUILT IN MY KITCHEN.

352. THE LOVE I HAVE FOR COOKING IS PALPABLE IN EACH DISH.

353. I AM A MASTER IN THE KITCHEN.

354. I AM ABLE TO CREATE ANYTHING THAT I DESIRE.

355. I AM BLESSED TO HAVE A WARM PLACE TO PREPARE MY MEALS.

356. I HAVE EVERYTHING I NEED TO MAKE WONDERFUL, NUTRITIOUS MEALS RIGHT HERE.

357. I AM VERY FORTUNATE TO BE ABLE TO EAT FOODS THAT HELP ME MAINTAIN MY OPTIMUM HEALTH.

358. I CAN SIMPLY PREPARE HEALTHY YET TASTY MEALS.

359. I AM DESERVING OF THE TIME AND MONEY I DEVOTE TO MY HEALTH.

360. I AM SO BLESSED TO BE ABLE TO PROVIDE MY FAMILY NUTRITIOUS CUISINE.

361. I AM PROUD OF THE FOOD I PREPARE AND SERVE.

362. MY MEALS OFFER JOY TO EVERYONE WHO EATS THEM.

363. I AM GRATEFUL FOR THE FRESH FRUITS AND VEGGIES USED IN MY MEALS.

364. I USE COOKING AS A CREATIVE OUTLET.

365. I USE COOKING AS A WAY TO GIVE BACK AND SHOW LOVE.

IF YOU ENJOYED THIS BOOK. KINDLY LEAVE A REVIEW ON AMAZON.

CHECKOUT MORE BOOKS ON AMAZON AT INSPIRE TODAY PRESS.

BLACK WOMEN SELF CARE ACTIVITY BOOK

notes

_____

_____

_____

_____

_____

_____

_____

_____

_____

_____

_____

notes

notes

_____

_____

_____

_____

_____

_____

_____

_____

_____

_____

_____

_____

notes

notes

_____

_____

_____

_____

_____

_____

_____

_____

_____

_____

_____

notes

_____

_____

_____

_____

_____

_____

_____

_____

_____

_____

_____

_____

notes

_____

_____

_____

_____

_____

_____

_____

_____

_____

_____

_____

_____

notes

_____

_____

_____

_____

_____

_____

_____

_____

_____

_____

_____

_____

_____

notes

_____

_____

_____

_____

_____

_____

_____

_____

_____

_____

_____

_____

Printed in Great Britain
by Amazon

35482356R00062